Save Money: 51 Money Saving Tips You Can Implement Right Away

By: Tracy Edwards

ISBN-13: 978-1482378054

Other Recommended Books:

Juicing Delicious Juice Recipes for Optimum Health (Optimum Health Series)

Annihilation - Utter Destruction (Annihilation, Book 1)

TABLE OF CONTENTS

PUBLISHERS NOTES
Disclaimer

This publication is intended to provide helpful and informative material. It is not intended to diagnose, treat, cure, or prevent any health problem or condition, nor is intended to replace the advice of a physician. No action should be taken solely on the contents of this book. Always consult your physician or qualified health-care professional on any matters regarding your health and before adopting any suggestions in this book or drawing inferences from it.

IMT, LLC is a publishing company and not a licensed financial advisor. All material published in this book is not intended to influence any decisions that you make and should not be construed as such. IMT, LLC, it's authors, owners, officers or partners do not hold itself out as providing any legal, financial or other advice. debt reduction plan in this book may not be suitable for you. If you have any doubts you should contact an independent financial advisor. The material in this book does not constitute advice and you should not rely on any material in this book to make (or refrain from making) any decision or take (or refrain from making) any action. Any action taken on your part will solely be your decision to act and IMT, LLC, its authors, owners, officers or partners will not be held responsible for your actions. IMT, LLC always recommends you seek the advice of a financial professional before taking any action on financial matters that could possibly affect you. This book is for informational purposes only. Results can vary depending on each individual's circumstances, amount of debt, level of action taken, and many other factors.

Paperback Edition 2013

Manufactured in the United States of America

DEDICATION

This book is dedicated to all the hard working people that can't seem to find enough money at the end of the month. It is my goal to help people find easy ways to save money and get out of debt.

FOREWORD

I have purposely created this book to be short in nature so it will be a quick read. I purposely made the cost very inexpensive so that anyone truly interested in taking back his or her lives can afford it.

There is no doubt in my mind the cost of this book can provide you with an ROI (return on invest) within your first month of implementing some of these techniques.

You will then want to take the ideas you feel will work for your specific situation and start implementing them to see some quick savings.

Once you get through the book you will probably start thinking of more and more ideas or ways you can come up with other money saving ideas of your own. Money saving can become addictive in nature once you see you have hope of getting out of debt.

If you have children it would be an ideal time to start teaching them about how to save money and make it a fun game. Have your children see who can come up with the most money saving ideas. This can teach your children that saving money can be just as much fun as spending it on toys.

It is reported that only 4% of the world's population is truly debt-free. With that being said, I knew there was a need to create this book, which can help individuals and families find enough money to start digging themselves out of debt once and for all.

It is sometimes strange to me why our education system doesn't teach individuals how to make money, save our money and live a debt free lifestyle. It is so simple once it is explained to you. I reiterate simple not always easy. I will be creating a book that will go into more detail on the techniques of getting anyone out of debt once and for all if they implement the techniques. For now I thought it would be better to get these money saving techniques in your hand so you can start coming up with more money each month to apply to your debts.

If you are one of the individuals that have conquered debt, you may want to employ some of these money-saving techniques to increase your monthly money savings plan.

My goal was to create a book that will truly make a difference in individuals lives that are buried in debt and do not see a way to break free. I too was once in this position, but implemented many of the strategies outlined in this book to a debt-free way of thinking and living.

My family and I were buried in so much debt. I never believed for a second that we would ever be free from debt or have any savings. I was determined to find a way out and started searching in all of our spending areas. My goal changed to purchasing things cheaper, to eliminating waste, limiting spending to only purchasing things that were needed.

I was able to locate several hundred dollars a month in savings to start applying it to my credit card with the least amount of debt. From there, as one bill was paid off I would then take the minimum amounts I was paying on that credit card and add it to the next bill with the least amount of debt. I continued the process until all unsecured debt was paid off. Once these credit cards were paid off it had increased my monthly savings into an amount in the thousands. I then started taking the thousands of dollars a month and applying it to our mortgage until it was also paid off.

I know this book is powerful if you decide to take action and implement its contents. If you are serious about finding money savings techniques then I'm sure you will find this book is just what you are you looking for. I wish you all the best in your quest to finally achieve a debt free life.

CHAPTER 1- SAVING MONEY IN A TRYING ECONOMY

Many people are asking, "How can I get out of debt in this economy?" The answer lies in this short, easy-to-implement book. Find out how to reduce your debt by cutting everyday costs and putting that money towards your debts. This book is going to give you 51 ideas to save your money as well as get your creative juices flowing so you can come up with your own ideas on how to save even more money.

Let's face it; with the economy in the tank, gas prices going through the roof, possibility of not having social security when you retire, pensions disappearing, you say what's a pension? Oh yea, that is what companies used to offer employees after they retired wherein they would give you a percentage of your yearly earnings for the rest of your life, usually in a monthly payment.

You see times have greatly changed and more and more financial responsibility lies on the individual. We have to start living under our own means so that we can save for the future, our kid's future, retirement and any other extra dreams you may have like traveling to Europe, sitting with your loved one at a café, sipping that espresso, and listening to the bell ring at the church in the center of town.

These dreams will be only a dream if we as individuals continue to live above our own means.

One thing this simple book will provide is 101 tips to help you immediately start saving money on purchases you are already making and move you into a mindset of saving money. Once you save the money, actually take the money and put it into a separate bank account. This brings me to debt reduction principles that actually work.

DEBT REDUCTION PRINCIPLES THAT ACTUALLY WORK

Pennies add up to dollars and dollars add up to multiple dollars. With a little time or once a month apply those savings to the smallest debt you have while maintaining your other minimum payments.

With time you will be applying the same principles that keep you enslaved to debt. In the beginning you will slowly reduce your debt, but this is where you don't want to give up and slip back into buying unnecessary items.

Once your first debt is paid off you now want to take that monthly payment and all the extra savings and now apply it to the next lowest balance.

For example,

Credit Card 1: Let's say you have a credit card debt with $5,000 and a minimum monthly payment of $500.

Credit Card 2: Has a credit card debt of $3,000 with a minimum monthly payment of $300.

Credit Card 3: Has a credit card debt of $1,000 with a minimum monthly payment of $100.

You would take your extra savings, for example purpose let's use a savings of $50 a month and apply it to the $1,000 credit card, which would increase your payment to $150 dollars reducing the principle, another $50.00 a month. You would only pay the minimum balance on the $5,000 and $3,000 credit cards. Once the $1,000 credit card is paid in full you would take the minimum payment ($100 + $50 = $150) along with the extra monthly saving and apply them to credit card debt 2.

So, for example purpose we would apply the $100 + $50 = $150 to credit card 2 along with the minimum payment of credit card 2. It would look like this $100 from minimum payment from credit card 3 (now paid off so the money is freed up) + $50 (extra savings) + $300 minimum credit card payment from credit card 2.

$100 +$50 + $300 = $450 a month applied to credit card 2.

So, now if we stick to our guns and don't add any new debt with the above example we would be able to pay off credit card 2 within 7 months. You would then do the same process for credit card 1 once credit card 2 is paid off.

$100 + $50 + $300 + $500 = $950 a month applied to credit card 1.

Now you are snow balling the debt and are reducing debt at a much faster rate than the beginning of our process. With the above example $5,000 / $950 a month payment you could have that credit card paid off in only 6 months.

Can you see the power behind taking those savings and compounding them in your favor to reduce debt? The process you are now implementing is the same process the unsecured debt is using against you, but you are now smarter and using compounding to your advantage to get out of debt.

Once smaller debts are erased, you can use the savings to reduce other debts like your home or save all the freed up money for retirement or your kid's college.

It is imperative that you decide not to incur any other debt so you can start the process of getting out of debt. It can be a smart decision to close your credit cards once the debt is eliminated to avoid having access to so much open credit. I would only keep your best credit card with the lowest rates open for a real emergency issue that may arise. Keeping one credit card open will also help you feel like you have a backup plan in a true emergency. I can't stress this enough though, **ONLY USE THE CREDIT CARD FOR EMERGENCYS!** Making un-necessary purchases again will cause your total debt reduction plan to be extended. Extending your debt elimination date can cause you to lose thousands of dollars in future investment dollars and delay being truly financially free. This leads me to the number one reason people stay in debt called Lack of Determination.

CHAPTER 2- HAVE DETERMINATION AND STICK WITH YOUR PLAN

If you truly want to conquer debt and become debt free you must have determination to succeed or the tips in this book on how to save money won't help you. You have to have a big enough **REASON! A WHY!** Something that is more important to you than staying in the vicious debt cycle. Once you determine your reason you will find more strength to follow through and accomplish your goal to become debt free.

I recommend sitting down in a quiet place with your partner, if married, or significant other and determine what is your big enough reason to stay focused until you achieve debt freedom. If you don't find a strong enough reason, you probably won't follow through and this book will only add to your debt.

Every person is different and may have a different reason that burns deep inside them. It could be that you don't want to work until your 80 years old welcoming people to Wal-Mart. Don't get me wrong there is nothing wrong with type of job or working into your later years, but you may want to have the choice. You may want to provide for your kids college and know if you continue down the debt path you won't have enough to help them. You may want to have a better quality of living when retiring and traveling to your ideal secluded locations or taking the cruise of a lifetime.

If you determine that gut level, burning desire and make it a daily goal you can overcome the urge to spend excessively. You now have a more important goal, the goal to be financially debt free and that you are determined you are going to reach because you see an end in sight. You may only be months away from eliminating your debt and setting your life up for financial freedom. Only you can determine how far you want to go.

I will say this, and many others will agree saving money can become addictive. Once you start saving and see those debts being erased you will probably start thinking of other ways to save even more money or start a small no or low cost business that will produce even more money to help get out of debt even quicker.

The following are simple ideas that can help you save more money and if applied to your debts, can create a debt free lifestyle.

CHAPTER 3- SAVE MONEY ON FOOD

Let's face it we all have to eat, right? Well in the area of food, there is a lot of room for savings. Grocery shopping to eating out can take a big chunk out of a person's budget. Here are some great ideas for saving more money in this area.

1. A grocery store is not created equal. You can find everything from top priced grocery stores to discount grocery stores. Think about it, off brand grocery items are created somewhere right? Well a lot of the time the can goods are created at the same locations as those high priced can good distribution centers, but just have the labels changed. The food is still the same quality but the price can be greatly reduced due to less overhead and marketing.

2. Find a discount-shopping network like Sam's or Costco. They offer lower prices when you buy in bulk. If your family consumes a lot of a specific type of food, it may save a lot if you buy

those items in bulk. Example: Cereal, if your family consumes a lot of cereal you may want to look at the savings of buying cereal in bulk. Other examples would be toilet paper, paper towels, dog food, dog treats, coffee, produce, milk, eggs etc.

3. Never go to the grocery store when you're hungry. It is proven that if you're hungry, you tend to purchase more unneeded items you may not have purchased if you weren't hungry. Let's face it, everything sounds good when we're hungry and we tend to overspend when we are shopping while hungry.

4. Make a list before shopping. You can save a lot of money by only purchasing grocery items that are needed and on your list. If it's not on your list don't buy it. Grocery stores place some of the highest priced items eye level for kids and impulse purchases close to the cash register, hoping you'll see it and grab those last minute items at the register.

5. Watch for your local grocery store flyers. Take each flyer and compare the specials for that week. You may have to go to more stores but can reduce your food bill by buying the items needed on sale.

6. Stock up on the sale items while they are discounted. Try and buy a month or two's worth of these products.

7. Compare the unit price of items to similar items to determine the lowest price.

8. Fruits and Vegetables can become expensive. Purchase your fruits and vegetables in season for the lowest price. I know blueberries are very expensive in off-season. When the blueberries are in season the price drops and they provide you with a larger quantity. You may also want to look at purchasing frozen fruits that are sometimes cheaper than fresh fruits.

9. Ask for a rain check if the sales items are sold out so you can save money when they get more in stock.

10. Most grocery stores have a discount isle for slightly damaged goods. Always look in this isle for items on your list.

11. Stay away from boxed and convenience foods. These items are more expensive than foods you can cook. Shopping the outer isles of the store can provide the healthiest foods, which tend to also be cheaper. Shopping the inner isles are where the higher price, less healthy boxed meals are located.

12. Purchase your non-food items at discount retail store like Sam's, Costco, Wal-Mart, Target etc. They are usually cheaper than purchasing them at the grocery store.

13. Look for a local butcher shop to purchase your meat. Local butchers often offer lower prices than retail chain grocery stores and

some offer meat raised in your local area. Healthier meats come from free-range farms and that aren't feed corn or injected with hormones. They are allowed to graze on the grass and tend to have less stress making the meat much healthier.

14. Locate a local cattle farmer and go in with a friend to purchase a half of cow. You can decide how you want to the cow processed for your meat needs. You can pick ground beef, roast, steak etc. You may need an extra freezer to store the cow but there is huge savings in this tip.

15. Locate a local pig farmer and purchase 1 or 2 pigs. You can have the pig made into whatever types of meat you enjoy such as sausage, bacon or ham.

16. Once you locate a grocery store, inquire about a loyalty discount program that can save you money. The loyalty discount program can

provide additional discounts when shopping at that store.

17. Keeping track of prices from the different stores can help you determine a bargain when you see it.

18. If you're lucky to have a farmers market or roadside stand, stop by one to pick up fresh fruits and vegetables. The prices are usually lower and you can negotiate a cheaper price. It may help if you become a regular before attempted a discounted price.

19. Be sure to ask your store if they run any specials on certain days like Thursday is double coupon day, or specials on day old bread etc. and plan you're shopping around this day.

20. Figure out a grocery budget and stick to it. If your family is fed easily on $200 a week, don't spend a penny more. Stay within the budget you set.

21. Once you have your budget amount, take that amount out of your bank account and save it in an envelope as cash. Now only buy groceries with your cash envelope. Plan your purchases to get the most meals with your grocery budget. When the money is gone for the week stop buying.

22. When purchasing chicken, purchase the chicken with the skin still on it. Skinless chicken is almost always more due to them removing the skin.

23. Save money by purchasing deli meats and cheeses from the dairy case instead of the deli. The deli prices tend to be higher than the dairy case.

24. Look for in store coupons. While shopping, some grocery stores have coupons for certain items sticking out from the shelves. Simply pick a coupon up while selecting the items.

25. Store checkouts may not always be accurately scanning your sale items. Watch the register while your items are being rung up to avoid overpaying for an item.

26. Now that you purchased your items check the receipt before leaving and make sure all coupons were applied correctly along with sale items.

CHAPTER 4 – SAVING WITH COUPONS

Coupons are a great way to save a lot of money over the course of a year. Staying dedicated to clipping them and using them every time you shop can add up to some great savings.

27. Sign up to a coupon club or newsletter. They will usually send coupons to you via email once or twice a month depending on the company. You can simply search "Coupons" in your search bar and come up with thousands of website that offer free coupons on groceries, clothing, dinning out, and just about anything you can think of.

28. Start a coupon swap with friends and family members. Swap coupons you don't use with coupons you do use.

29. Check with your grocery store to find out if they have specific days for double or triple coupon days. Shop accordingly.

30. When you enter the store always check there in store coupon magazine. There are coupons in there that aren't always in the weekly sales flyer.

31. Contact all manufactures that you purchase products from and inquire if they have a coupon program. If so, asked to be put on their mailing or email list for additional coupons.

32. Check and see if your community has local coupon mailers and get on their lists. There are usually several good coupons inside one mailer.

33. Try and save your coupons and use them when your items you purchase go on sale to get a super saver discount.

34. Use a coupon organizer to achieve the best results with coupons. Staying organized and using the coupons before they expire will save you money.

Extreme couponing has become so popular that there is now a show about it. Some of those individuals get so good they purchase over a thousand dollars of groceries for a small fee or some can zero out the register. If you want to become this good with couponing I want you to know it takes some time and preparation finding the coupons, clipping them, organizing them which could take several hours a week to accomplish. It could become a part-time job, but if you have the time this could save you hundreds to thousands of dollars per month.

CHAPTER 5- SAVE MONEY BY EATING AT HOME

Eating at home is another great way to save money. Why is it cheaper to eat at home? The greatest cost when we eat out is that someone else is preparing our meals and they get a premium price for that service. So, when you do the prep work and cook your meals yourself, you save that cost. Remember you can also eat a much healthier meal when you make it yourself.

35.   Eating at home can save a lot of money over the course of a year. Let's face it, it's much easier to pick something up while you're out and not have to cook, no prep time, just eat and pay. Well you're losing a lot of your budget if you're eating out very much.

36.   Cook meals ahead for the week. This will save time and have home cooked meals easily accessible. Meals can quickly be ready to eat while saving money.

37. Gather several recipes that afford you quick, easily prepared meals. This can keep you out of the drive thru and more money in your pocket.

38. Most families have their pantries filled with items. Try not shopping for a week and eat whatever you have in your pantry. Take the grocery shopping money for that week and put it in your savings account. Big savings.

39. Bringing your lunch to work can really add up to some great savings. If you eat out every day that can get expensive. By bringing your already prepared meals you may save as much as $5.00-$10.00 a day and eat a healthier meal.

40. When shopping in discount, wholesale clubs be sure to pick up some snack foods you enjoy. Add these to your lunch bag so you can avoid overpaying at the vending machine.

41. Clean out your freezer by eating what's in it. You can cut your grocery bill again by eating up the freezer food before it gets freezer burn and you have to throw it out.

42. Make one day a week pick it night. Combine all the leftovers and pick out separate meals for the family. This way you will not have to throw away any food and you will have gotten the biggest bang for your buck.

43. For other snack ideas, buy chips and pretzels in bigger bags and bring some of your favorite's snacks in a zip lock bag. Definitely cheaper than the vending machine.

44. Create a soup and salad night or a vegetarian casserole night to cut down on the expensive meat purchases.

45. If you enjoy gardening, plant your own tomatoes, cucumbers, lettuce, corn, etc. to save even more on your grocery bill. You'll have organic grown produce you grew without the

harmful pesticides. You may even have fun watching over your garden.

46. Instead of buying an expensive cup of coffee on your drive to work, you can usually purchase your favorite coffee at your discount club for way less. Simply brew your own Starbuck, Dunkin Donuts, etc. from home. This one tip alone can save a lot of money in just one week.

47. If you're really thrifty you can mix your favorite premium coffee with regular coffee. Simply mix the premium coffee 3 parts to 1 part regular coffee. This will make the premium coffee go even further without a loss of flavor.

48. Stock up on your favorite ice cream or frozen treats instead of buying it from the ice cream truck. You'll always have your children's favorite treat on hand when they hear the ice cream man, but you're saving money while giving them what they want.

49. Create some meals from scratch when possible. These meals are not only healthier but also much cheaper than drive thru meals and convenient box meals.

50. Purchase a bread machine and make your own healthy bread from scratch without the unwanted added ingredients from store bought bread. Your house will smell great.

51. If your fruits start to expire, get creative and make banana bread, or a strawberry desert cup. The idea here is to not have any waste. Consume everything you purchase. This will save you money over time.

CHAPTER 6 - CONCLUSION

This book was created for individuals that can't seem to find any extra money and are hurting financially. Most families that implement these simple saving strategies can save hundreds to thousands of dollars a year.

This book is a simple system, and if implemented will help you get started on saving money right away. There are 51 ideas to kick start your savings plan. Hopefully this book will spark something deep inside you to see the endless possibilities for savings.

We all have options put before us each and every day. Do you have a strong enough why a strong enough reason to take over your financial life.

Dig deep, do some soul searching. Don't put off this part of the plan. I'm sure you've heard the saying

<u>"You don't plan to fail, you simply fail to plan!"</u>
(Writer Unknown).

Don't wake up looking to retire and be buried in debt. If you don't take action now, then when will you? Carpi Diem (seize the day). If you want to ever get out of debt and become financially free you have to eliminate debt. The sooner you start your plan the sooner you can get out of debt and start saving for retirement or other personal desires.

None of us wake up and plan to fail we just get busy and tell ourselves we are going to start saving some day in the near future. Well I'm here to tell you that every day you fail to plan you are losing out on money you could be saving for your future.

Debt is expensive and causes so much pain and anxiety in individuals and families' lives. Banks and credit card companies are the ones making the money. They love to offer low minimum payments because each month they are making millions of dollars. They love for you to pay only the minimum; it keeps you paying them interest, which is pure, profit every month you make a payment.

If you stay on their minimum payment plan you can plan on paying that debt for years and that's without putting any additional purchases on your credit card. Paying for items this way can cost you hundreds if not thousands of extra dollars over you're original purchase price.

The key is thinking a little differently and finding where the money is leaking out of your savings and then fill the holes. The faster you fill the holes and use the new found savings to pay down your debts, the quicker you can start to accumulate wealth.

If you are serious about getting out of debt please find your why. If you have a family, sit down and talk about making a plan that everyone can agree on and implement it together.

Bringing your family together and agreeing on the program can really build a great support group for when times get tough. Support each other, make saving money fun and see who can save the most from their own ideas. When you make it fun it becomes enjoyable.

If you aren't really wanting to save money and it becomes a chore, well, you probably will not follow the program very long, give up and go right back to spending more than your making, growing your debt bigger and bigger.

Let's think through that for a minute. In a few more years is it going to be harder or easier to get out of the hole? Harder right? So, today is the first day of the rest of your life.

Your future is in your hands. It may seem like a daunting task right now, but if you implement this simple program you will shortly see how much money you can save and apply to your debts.

So guys please, please, please find your why. Sit down and brainstorm ideas to save money, put this books savings plan to use. Get with your loved ones to share more ideas. Then above all take action!! Put your plan into an actionable plan. Start your plan today and don't wait until tomorrow because it will be costing a lot more money in the long run.

I truly want you to become successful and enjoy a debt free life. It just takes determination that you will be one of the few who dedicate themselves to taking action. If you take action on these principles you will succeed.

SAVING WHEN DEBT FREE

If you are already debt free, I would like to applaud you. You are in a small percentage of people in the United States. You have found your why, your reason and have been disciplined to accomplish the task of becoming debt free.

If you are already debt free, please use the ideas in this book to compound your savings. It may spark new ideas for you save even more money per month adding more money to your net worth.

One of my financial advisers once told me it was easier to hold on to the money you have already made than it is to make more. This theory still holds true, especially in this economy.

Another little comment is what changed my life. I never thought about money like this before. He stated, "If you spend everything you make your still broke."

He gave me a couple of made up scenarios and then hit me with this:

If medical doctor X makes $200,000 dollars a year and his/her bills consume all the money they make, they are still broke. They may have fancier toys and homes but if their net worth is $0.00, their still BROKE!

There are also individuals that make a modest living making $40,000 household income but have saved money and live a debt free life style with $400,000 in investments. So, in this scenario who is the person with the most wealth?

He went on to say it is not how much money you make but how much money you save and invest wisely that will give you a secure future. So, no matter the amount of money you make, you need to live below your means in order to save for the future.

I left his office kind of in shock, but his words rang true to my spirit. I saw something that day that opened my eyes and learned that anyone can become financially independent if they truly wanted to. I figured out quickly that day, the choice lies within each of us.

Hopefully this book can help you take your financial future back into your control and not the big credit card companies, mortgage companies and businesses.

I hope you enjoyed this book and that it has sparked something deep inside you to take action and make the necessary changes to start saving your hard earned money.

I know the content of this book has changed my future. It has given many others and me a feeling of true freedom. Remember true freedom comes from owning your life and not being indebted to others.

Once you accomplish a debt free style of living, you truly will be one of the top 4% of the people in the world and will have accomplished something that most people only dream about. I can't tell you enough how liberating a debt free life can be. To wake up in the morning and feel that a pressure is gone, the stress lifted, and knowing now you can invest for your future.

I am working on my next book, which will be going into more details on how to use your newfound money savings to help eliminate your debts. In my next book, I will cover tips and techniques that I have used to accelerate my debt reduction in the fastest amount of time. I truly want to provide value and want to work with individuals that are looking for a better way of life than to be indebted. I want for you what I now have in my life, freedom.

Once again I'd like to thank you for your purchase of this book. I hope you enjoyed it and it has opened your eyes to how important it is to save money and get out of debt. The decision lies inside each and every individual. Find your why and take action, you'll thank yourself once you did.

I was devastated when my debt grew to over six figures. Our real estate investments tanked, business expenses were put on our credit cards and we started sinking fast.

Two short sales, a bankruptcy, and several years of stress took its toll on my family and I's lives.

I started formulating a debt elimination plan that is still in full force today. My family has paid off all debts minus our mortgage, which is quickly diminishing.

I know how much our family was hurting while we were in debt, how little extra money there was at the end of the month. We were struggling to find enough money to provide for our family's needs.

Tracy Edwards

I decided it was my new passion to get out of debt and build wealth. If my techniques worked for my family, I knew they would work for others.

I couldn't sit by with critical information that could help others take back their lives and financial futures.

So, I decided to write a book that lays out the very simple techniques we used to become debt free from credit cards, car loans, and eventually our home.

In the book you will learn how to pay off your debts including your mortgage in just a handful of years. I discovered by simple math that this is the fastest way to reduce debts and build wealth.

You'll be surprised to learn why it's not your fault you're in debt.

Why continuing to pay off your mortgage early and before starting to invest can leave you with more than a million dollars in the same time period.

Let's face it guys; we are not taught in school or anywhere else how to take financial responsibility and achieve financial prosperity.

You'll also discover why those marketing tricks, such as "low, easy to afford monthly payments" or "limited quantities, be sure and purchase today before supplies run out" are just great marketers stealing your financial future.

The program had to be easy for me to follow in order to stick with it. There is no real "Budget" if you will, to follow. Just a little education combined with a simple to follow plan that is actionable. That's it!

I'm sure that anyone who truly wants to eliminate debt and build wealth can do it. You do have to take action and be determined for a handful of years to totally eliminate your debts.

If this sounds like something you're struggling with, then watch for my next book.

You must decide to take action, stay motivated and apply the techniques to receive the results your desire.

If you decide to purchase any of my books and feel you received value, could I ask you a big favor? Would you do me a favor and go back to by book in Amazon Kindle or Amazon for physical books and leave me a positive review.

It is truly my goal to provide value for individuals that purchase my books. If you feel like my books have provided value I would appreciate you leaving an honest review on my Amazon book page.

Your review may be the deciding factor that helps someone else that needs help, decide to purchase my books and give them a better quality of life.

Thank you again for putting your faith in my books and me.

I would like to wish you all the best in your lives and tell you that I believe in you. Stay dedicated to your goals and a debt reduction program and you will achieve your financial dreams.

My true goal in life is to help people change their lives for the better, one person at a time.

I wish you all the best. Here's to your success!

Tracy Edwards

BACKLIST: OTHER RECOMMENDED BOOKS:

To get your copy, simply go to Amazon.com or click the link below:

Smoothies: 25 Healthy Smoothie Recipes for Better Health (Optimum Health Series)

www.ingramcontent.com/pod-product-compliance
Lightning Source LLC
Chambersburg PA
CBHW051246170526
45165CB00004B/1596